IF ALIENS ARE TRYING TO A...
ALL YOU NEED IS WHAT'S FOR DINNER? TO SURVIVE!

Use the magazine as a shield to protect yourself from the aliens' laser beams.

Roll the magazine up and use it to swat at the aliens like a fly swatter.

Rip out pages and crumple them up to throw at the aliens as makeshift weapons.

Use the magazine as a bargaining chip to negotiate your release from the aliens.

Use the magazine as a distraction and sneak away while the aliens are flipping through the pages.

Hey there, grown-ups!

I am excited to have you here as we embark on a journey together to explore the beautiful practice of prayer. You have already taught your kids how to walk, talk, and handle various challenges along the way. Now, I invite you to help them explore the art of being present with God.

The practice of prayer is truly one of the most precious gifts we can pass on to our children, and it will last a lifetime. Imagine the impact of having a child who knows they can turn to God in times of need, who seeks His guidance when making decisions, and who finds solace in His presence during difficult times. By teaching our children to pray, we are instilling in them a foundation of faith that will sustain them throughout their lives.

This issue of *What's for Dinner?* is designed to support you in this important journey. I hope that all the activities and practical tips will help you guide your children in developing a vibrant prayer life. I believe that prayer should be a joyful and meaningful experience for children, and our magazine is here to make that happen.

So, let's embark on this exciting adventure of nurturing a deep and personal connection between our children and God. Together, let's give them the gift of prayer—an invaluable treasure that will enrich their lives and shape their hearts for eternity.

Dema Kohen
What's for Dinner?
Editor-in-chief

Want to send this magazine to a friend? Order more copies at **WhatsForDinnerMag.com**

HOW TO PRAY

Prayer is one of God's greatest gifts to you! You are able to speak directly to Him — the great God of the universe — anytime, anywhere. Stop and think about that . . . you are talking to this great big God who made the world and made you, the God who placed the stars in the sky and brings the sun up every morning. That is quite a thought!

PRAISES
Thank God for who He is and what He has done for you, and tell Him what you love about Him.

REPENTANCE
Confess your sins and mess-ups, and receive God's forgiveness.

FEELINGS
Tell God what you're feeling. Pour out your worries, joys, fears, frustrations, and so on.

THOUGHTS
Tell God what's on your mind — your plans, dreams, questions, wonderings.

SILENCE
It's a good idea to spend a few moments quietly waiting for God to speak to you.

CONCERNS
Tell your Father in Heaven what you or other people need.

WOW!

CAN YOUR FAMILY IDENTIFY THE BIBLE STORY IN EACH LOST NOTICE?

LOST!

Paradise. The grass was definitely greener on the other side.

(Genesis 3:21-24)

LOST

One sheep. I still have ninety-nine, but I really want that one back.

(Luke 15:1-7)

My first love. La seen in the city o Ephesus.

(Revelation 2:1-7)

LOST

My strength. A foreign woman took it from me.

(Judges 16:6-18)

LOST

My voice. Last seen in the temple of the Lord.

(Luke 1:5-21)

LOST

My mind. Last seen on the roof of the royal palace.

(Daniel 4:28-37)

LOST

A 12-year-old boy. Answers to the name of Yeshua.

(Luke 2:41-50)

USE THE UPSIDE-DOWN REFERENCES IF YOU'RE NOT SURE.

LOST

My favorite son. Last seen wearing a special jacket I gave him.

(Genesis 37:23-24)

LOST

My sleep and appetite. Probably shouldn't have punished that innocent man.

(Daniel 6:18)

! LOST !

My eyesight. Last seen on the road to Damascus.

(Acts 9:1-9)

LOST !

My head. It happened after an unfortunate collision with a UFO.

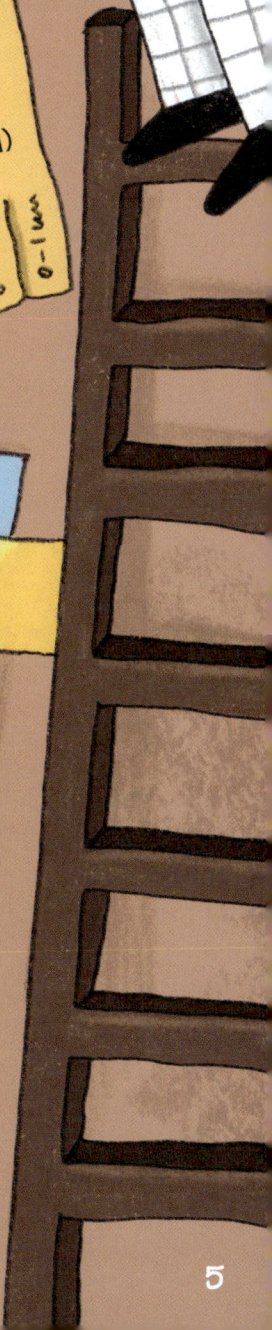

(1 Samuel 17:48:51)

THE UNEXPECTED

Jack had the best life any 8-year-old boy could ask for. He woke up every morning in his comfortable bed, surrounded by his favorite stuffed animals, with the sun peeking through his window.

His family lived in a little town nestled in a cozy spot between rolling hills and green fields. This town was so small that everyone knew each other, and you couldn't go to the store without bumping into an old friend.

Jack looked forward every day to going to school because he loved to learn and hang out with his friends.

When he wasn't at school, he and his buddies played soccer, rode bikes, fished in the pond, or searched for hidden treasure in the woods.

Most evenings, Jack's dad would play catch with him in the backyard and some nights they would lie on the soft warm grass looking at the clear sky and counting twinkling stars.

Jack's life was wonderful until the day his parents decided to move to the city for better job opportunities. Jack had to leave behind his school, friends, and everything he knew and loved.

ANSWER

BY DEMA KOHEN

Jack was devastated. He missed his old life and couldn't seem to adjust to his new surroundings.

He missed all the twinkling stars and the chirping crickets at night. He missed the fresh dew in the morning and the feeling of the country air in his lungs. He would often picture himself jumping into the pond or running through a field. But more than anything, he missed his friends.

He cried himself to sleep every night, asking God to take his family back to their "real" home, but it seemed as if God was silent.

Jack became more and more frustrated, and he started to feel that praying was useless.

One day, Jack was walking home from school, and he saw a stray dog wandering around. The poor animal was skinny, and his fur was matted and dirty. Jack felt pity for him, and he decided to take him home.

7

It became clear to him that God had been answering his prayers all along, just not in the way he expected.

When Jack's parents saw the dog, they were hesitant. They didn't want to take in a stray, but Jack begged and pleaded with them until they finally gave in.

Jack took good care of his new friend. He named him Buddy and fed, bathed, and played with him every day.

One day, while Jack was playing with Buddy, he realized that something had changed inside him. He no longer felt so alone or hopeless.

God hadn't taken away his circumstances but had given him a friend to walk through it with him.

That night, Jack prayed again. But this time, he didn't ask God to give him his old life back. Instead, he asked God to keep giving him the strength to get through the tough times and embrace the new beginning.

And as Jack drifted off to sleep, for the first time in months he felt a sense of peace. He knew that God was with him every step of the way.

EXPLORE TOGETHER

What is the biggest change you have ever experienced in life? Was it difficult?

Have you ever been surprised by the unexpected way God answered a prayer?

CREATE A PRAYER SPACE

TRY THIS AT HOME

Having a special place to connect with God can help improve your prayer life because it creates a calm and peaceful environment where you can focus better.

Here's how you can create a sacred space just for you and God to hang out together!

First, find a quiet spot or a cozy nook where you won't be disturbed.

Then, choose a few items that make you feel peaceful and happy, like a special pillow, a soft comfy blanket, or a beautiful painting. Add a battery-powered candle or some smooth rocks or green plants for a calming touch.

Next, spend some time in your sacred space every day. You can read a Bible story, say a prayer, or just sit quietly and listen for God's voice.

Remember, your prayer space can be anything you want it to be!

Just make it a place where you feel close to God and at peace. It will be like a secret hideout where you talk to God and listen to Him without any distractions, making your prayers stronger and more meaningful.

Take a photo of your prayer space and email it to us or share it on social media and tag *@whatsfordinnermag*

This *Jesus of Nazareth* doll could be a great addition to your prayer spot. See more pics in our online store.

WITH JESUS IN THE SCHOOL OF {PRAYER}

Did you know that Jesus is the greatest example of prayer?

Yes, that's right! He taught us so many wonderful things about talking to God. Let's dive in and explore some practical lessons we can learn from Jesus about prayer.

LESSON 1

Find a Quiet Place

Jesus often went to quiet places to pray.

In the Gospel of Luke, it says that Jesus would "slip away to remote places and pray" (Luke 5:16).

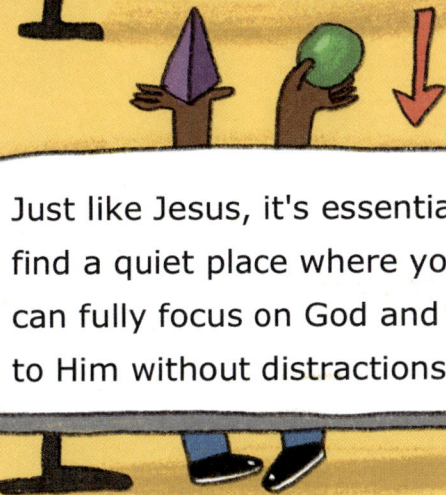

Can you think of a cozy spot where you can be alone with God?

Just like Jesus, it's essential to find a quiet place where you can fully focus on God and talk to Him without distractions.

LIFE APPLICATION

Next time you want to talk to God, find a calm spot in your house or backyard. Share your thoughts, joys, and concerns with your Heavenly Father. He's always listening!

LESSON 2

Pray with Thanksgiving

When Jesus prayed, He thanked God for His blessings.

In the Gospel of Matthew, it tells us how Jesus took five loaves of bread and two fish, looked up to heaven, and gave thanks to God (Matthew 14:19).

We can learn from Jesus to have a grateful heart and thank God for all the wonderful things He does for us.

LIFE APPLICATION

Before going to bed, think of three things you're grateful for. For example, your family, friends, pets, toys, a beautiful sunset, or even a delicious meal. Tell God about them and say, "Thank You, God, for [insert your blessings]."

Pray for Others

Jesus cared deeply for people, and He prayed for them too.

In the Gospel of John 17:9, Jesus prayed for His disciples.

We can follow Jesus' example by praying for our family, friends, and even our enemies.

In the Gospel of Luke 23:34, Jesus prayed for the people who crucified Him.

In the Gospel of Luke 22:32, Jesus prayed for Simon.

LIFE APPLICATION

Make a prayer list. Write down the names of people you want to pray for. Each day, choose someone from the list and say a special prayer for them. Your prayers will make a difference in their lives!

LESSON 4

Pray with Persistence

Jesus taught us to be persistent in prayer.

In the Gospel of Luke, Jesus tells a story about a widow who kept asking a judge for help (Luke 18:1-8).

Though the judge initially ignored her, he eventually granted her request because of her persistence.

Jesus teaches us that we should never give up when we pray but keep seeking God's help and guidance.

LIFE APPLICATION

Choose a specific prayer request that is close to your heart. Keep praying for it every day, even if it takes a long time to see an answer. Remember, God hears your prayers, and your persistence shows your faith and trust in Him. So, keep the faith, keep praying, and see how God works miracles in and through you.

Surrender to God's Will

One important lesson we can learn from Jesus is to surrender our desires to God's will.

In the Gospel of Matthew, Jesus prayed in the Garden of Gethsemane, saying, "Father, if it be possible, let this cup pass from me; nevertheless, not as I will, but as you will" (Matthew 26:39).

Jesus knew that God's plan was best, even if it meant facing difficult situations.

We can learn from Him to trust God's will for our lives.

LIFE APPLICATION
Whenever you pray, end your prayer by saying, "God, I trust Your plan for me." It's a way of surrendering your desires and asking God to guide you in His perfect way, just like Jesus did.

LESSON 6

Pray with Faith

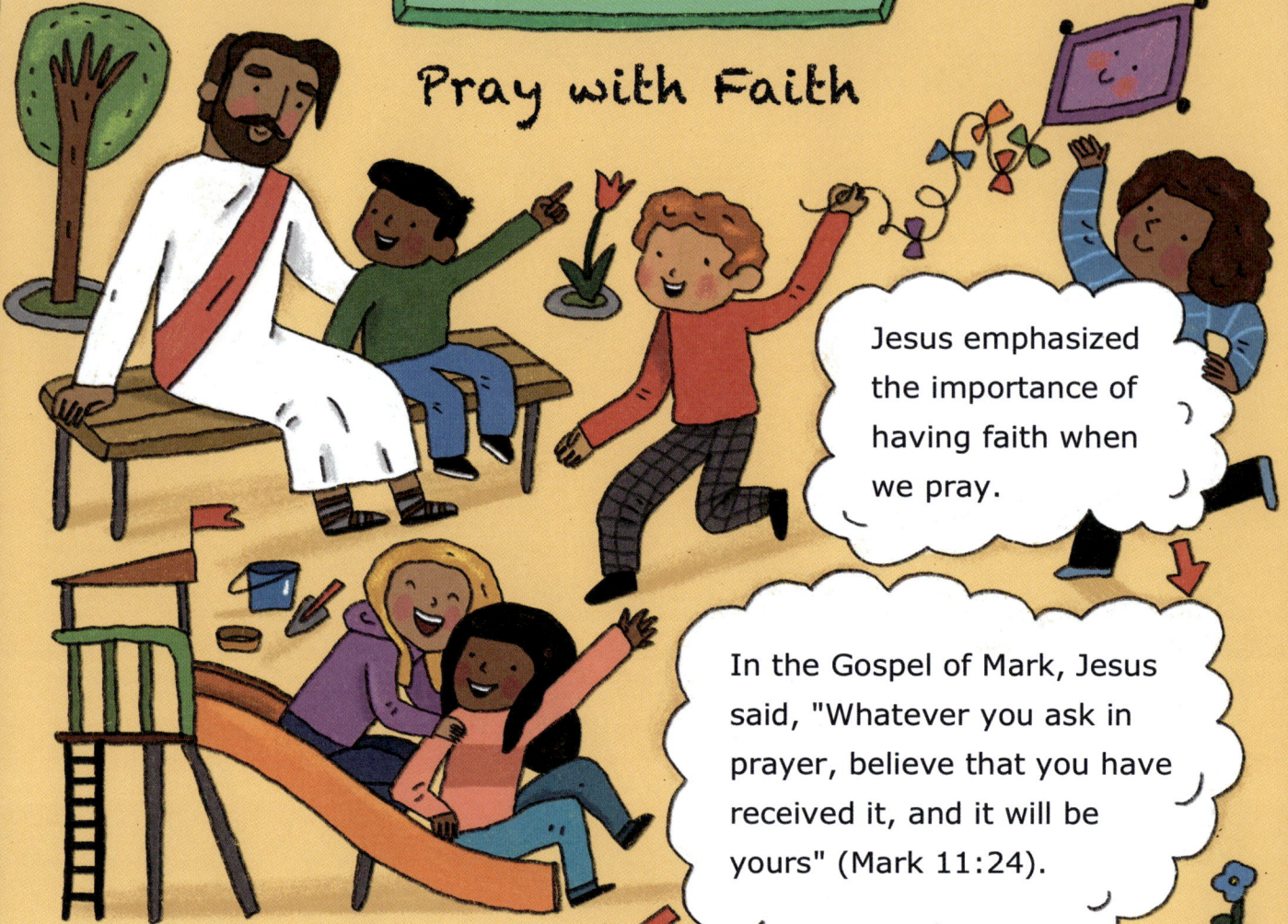

Jesus emphasized the importance of having faith when we pray.

In the Gospel of Mark, Jesus said, "Whatever you ask in prayer, believe that you have received it, and it will be yours" (Mark 11:24).

Jesus encouraged His disciples to have confidence in God's power and to believe that He would answer their prayers.

We can learn to pray with faith, knowing that God is listening and able to do great things.

LIFE APPLICATION

Choose a specific prayer request that seems impossible. Pray about it every day, but this time, add the phrase, "God, I believe You can do this!" Keep your eyes open for how God works in surprising ways.

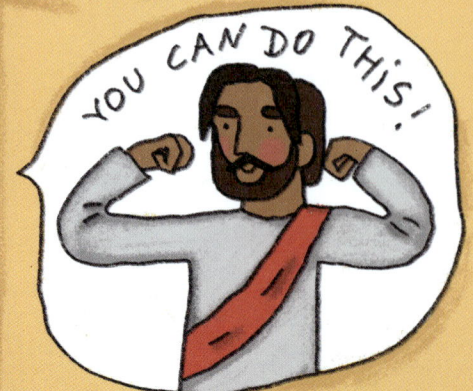

YOU CAN DO THIS!

LESSON 7

Pray with a Pure Heart

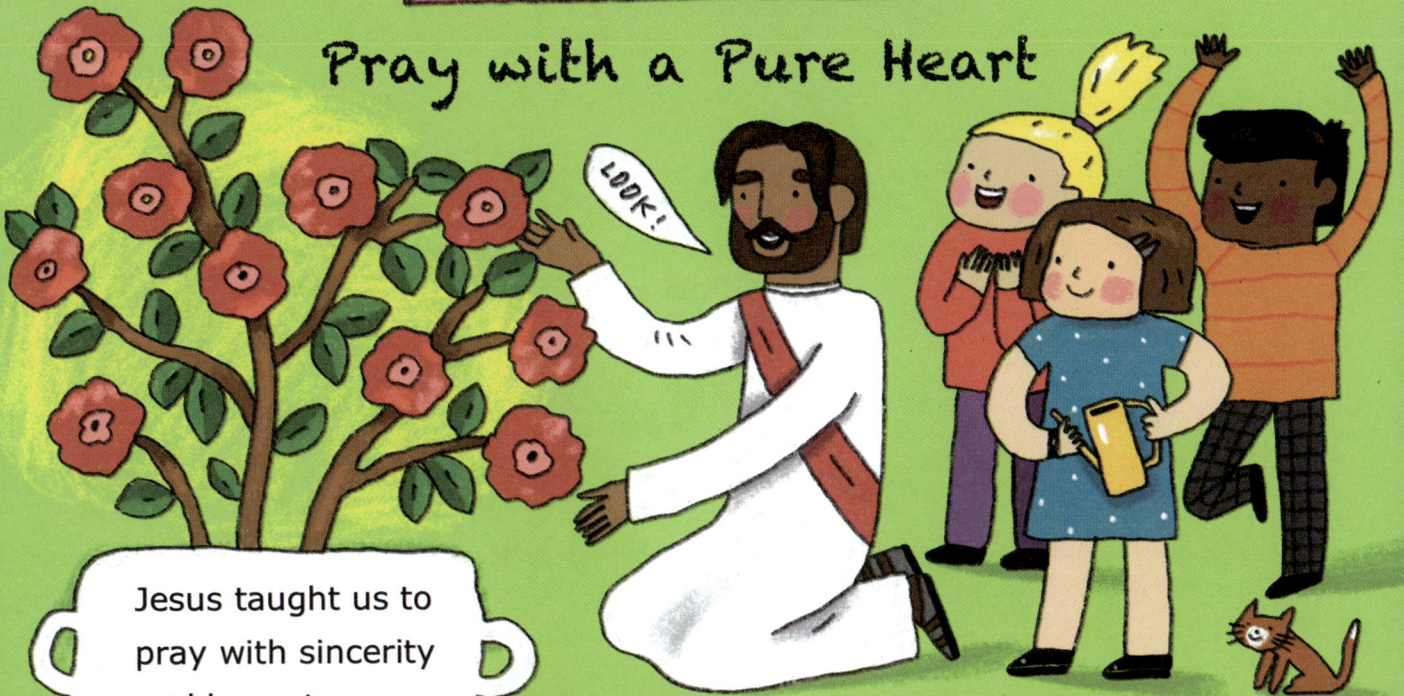

LOOK!

Jesus taught us to pray with sincerity and honesty.

In the Gospel of Matthew, He said, "And when you pray, do not heap up empty phrases as the Gentiles do, for they think that they will be heard for their many words" (Matthew 6:7).

Jesus wanted us to understand that prayer is not about fancy words or long speeches, but about having a genuine heart-to-heart conversation with God.

LIFE APPLICATION

When you pray, speak to God as if you're talking to a dear friend. Share your joys, fears, worries, and dreams openly and honestly. Remember, God loves you just the way you are, and He wants to hear from your heart!

Jesus showed us that prayer is not complicated or only for grown-ups. It's a special way to connect with God, talk to Him, and experience His love and guidance in our lives. So, let's follow in Jesus' footsteps and make prayer a part of our daily journey with Him.

PRAYER IN

The prayer of a righteous person is very powerful. (James 5:16)

Call to Me and I will answer you. (Jeremiah 33:3)

Never stop praying. (1 Thessalonians 5:17)

Keep on praying and guard your prayers with thanksgiving. (Colossians 4:2)

THE BIBLE

Don't worry about anything, but pray about everything. With thankful hearts offer up your prayers and requests to God. (Philippians 4:6)

Ask and it will be given to you; seek and you will find; knock and the door will be opened to you. (Matthew 7:7)

Is anyone among you in trouble? Let them pray. (James 5:13)

HOW STRONG iS YOUR PRAYER

Answer the following questions honestly and select the option that best describes your prayer life. At the end of the quiz, you will receive a score that reflects the strength of your prayer life. Remember, there are no right or wrong answers. Let's get started!

1 How often do you pray?

A) Every day, multiple times a day.

B) A few times a week.

C) Occasionally, when I need something.

D) Rarely or never.

2 Do you believe that God hears and answers your prayers?

A) Absolutely, without a doubt.

B) I hope so, but sometimes I doubt it.

C) Not sure, I've never really thought about it.

D) No, I don't think so.

RAWR!

3 What do you primarily pray about?

A) Everything, including praise, thanksgiving, and requests.

B) My family and friends.

C) Myself and my immediate needs.

D) I don't know, I just say words.

4 Do you spend time listening to God during prayer?

A) Yes, I make time to listen for His voice.

B) Sometimes, but it's hard to hear Him.

C) I never thought about listening to Him.

D) No, I didn't know you could listen to God.

LiFE?

5 How do you handle distractions during prayer?

A) I try to refocus and continue praying.

B) I get easily distracted and find it hard to concentrate.

C) I give up praying when distractions occur.

D) I don't get distracted because I don't pray much.

6 Do you pray for others?

A) I regularly pray for family, friends, and those in need.

B) I occasionally remember to pray for others.

C) I only pray for others when asked.

D) No, I only pray for myself.

7 Do you believe that your prayers are making a difference?

A) Yes, I believe that God hears and answers my prayers.

B) Sometimes, I'm not always sure if my prayers matter.

C) No, I don't think my prayers make a difference.

D) I haven't really thought about it.

8 How often do you pray with others (family, friends, church)?

A) Regularly, I enjoy praying together with others.

B) Occasionally, during specific events or gatherings.

C) Rarely, I prefer to pray alone.

D) I've never prayed with others.

9 Have you ever experienced answered prayers?

A) Yes, multiple times.

B) Once or twice, but not often.

C) I'm not sure if my prayers have been answered.

D) No, my prayers have never been answered.

10 How important is prayer in your daily life?

A) It's a vital part of my life, I can't imagine living without it.

B) It's important, but I sometimes forget to pray.

C) I don't think about prayer much.

D) Prayer is not important to me.

LET'S ADD UP YOUR SCORE!

For each question, assign the following points:

A) = 4 POINTS
B) = 3 POINTS
C) = 2 POINTS
D) = 1 POINTS

INTERPRETING THE SCORE:

35-40 POINTS
Your prayer life is strong! Keep nurturing your relationship with God through prayer.

25-34 POINTS
Your prayer life is developing. Seek opportunities to grow closer to God in prayer.

15-24 POINTS
Your prayer life needs improvement. Make an effort to prioritize prayer in your daily life.

10-14 POINTS
Your prayer life is weak. Take steps to strengthen your connection with God through prayer.

CREATE A PRAYER PLAYLIST

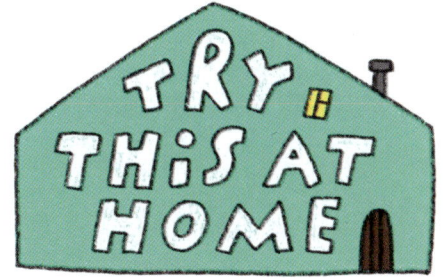

TRY THIS AT HOME

Have you ever felt like you wanted to pray but just didn't know how to start? Sometimes, it can be hard to connect with God and find the words to say. But don't worry, there's a simple solution – make a Prayer Playlist!

All you need to do is pick some of your favorite worship songs and add them to a playlist on a music streaming platform. Then, when you're feeling stuck or disconnected, play your playlist and let the music do the talking. The lyrics and melodies can help unlock your heart and allow your prayers to flow out.

Having a Prayer Playlist is like having a special tool that helps you talk to God. It can make a big difference in your prayer life and help you feel closer to Him. So, go ahead and create your own playlist with your caregivers' permission. You might just be surprised at how much it can help!

Ask your parents' permission to scan this QR code to listen to the Prayer Playlist we created for this issue of the magazine.

FLOWCODE
PRIVACY.FLOWCODE.COM

THE FAITHFUL DANIEL GAME

TO PLAY:

1 Place the game pieces on the START. The oldest person goes first and becomes the scorekeeper.

2 On your turn, toss a coin.
HEADS = move one space ahead.
TAILS = move two spaces ahead.

3 If you go to a space that's:

BLUE OR YELLOW:
All other players compete in the challenge. Set a timer for two minutes for players to draw or write. Let other players share their answers. Close your eyes while answers are turned in. Choose one at random. That person gets two points.

RED:
Do the action written on the space. Lose a point (if you have any.)

PURPLE:
Act out the scenario to earn a point.

GREEN:
Answer the question to earn a point.

4 The scorekeeper keeps track of all the points earned and lost.

5 The first player to reach FINISH earns five points. Once all players reach FINISH, the player with the most points wins!

YOU WILL NEED:

- A game piece for each player
- Pencils and crayons
- Scrap paper
- Timer
- Coin

GO!

START

TELL
Who do you know that followed God even when it cost them something?

DRAW
King Darius.

WRITE
How would you feel if you were in a den full of lions?

DID YOU KNOW?
Persia is modern-day Iran.

SCAN & WATCH

DID YOU KNOW?

The name Daniel means "God is my judge."

TELL

Who needs your prayers today?

DRAW

One rule in your life that's hard to obey/keep.

OH NO!

The statesmen convinced King Darius to outlaw praying. Recite The Lord's Prayer.

WRITE

Five boys' names start with that letter D.

ACT OUT

jealous statesmen spying on Daniel.

TELL

How do you pray when you don't have the words?

OH NO!

The jealous statesmen tattletaled on you to the King. Cry like a baby.

DRAW

A situation where it may be tough for you to follow God.

WRITE

A thank you note to someone in your family who has helped you feel brave recently.

OH NO!

Some men became jealous of you and decided to get rid of you. Make a sneaky face and let out evil laughter.

TELL

Do you lose heart and give up in prayer too quickly?

DRAW

Your favorite place to pray.

WRITE

The names of five people you want to pray for this week.

A-A-A

TELL
How vital is prayer in your life?

ACT OUT
Your reaction to seeing a lion in the wild, up close and personal.

DRAW
Daniel's face when he was tossed into the lion's den.

WRITE
Why do you suppose a lion is called "the king of the beasts"?

DRAW
Someone that you'd want to have by your side if you were thrown into a lion's den.

DID YOU KNOW?
Lions spend about 21 hours of their day just lying around sleeping.

WRITE
Three things that you are, have been, or scared of in your life.

TELL
Do you ever find prayer difficult?

ACT OUT
A hungry lion looking forward to his lunch.

OH NO!
The King ordered you to be thrown into the lions' den. Make a roaring sound like a lion.

ACT OUT
A time in your life when you were courageous.

DID YOU KNOW?
Lions can ea up to 88 pounds of meat in a single meal.

FLOWCODE
PRIVACY.FL

SCAN & WATCH

ACT OUT
A situation when you felt that God was with you.

WRITE
How does it make you feel to know that God is always with you?

DRAW
The face of King Darius when he found out Daniel was alive.

TELL
What is your prayer life like right now?

TELL
Do you ever wonder if God is really listening to your prayers?

FINISH

Z-Z-Z

DID YOU KNOW?
Lions are great tree climbers.

ACT OUT
How the angel of the Lord shut the mouths of the lions.

TELL
Do you struggle with feeling like God's not answering your prayers?

DRAW
The face of a hungry lion.

WRITE
About a time when you were afraid.

27

PRAYER QUOTES

" Prayer is the encounter of God's thirst with ours. God thirsts that we may thirst for Him. "

ST. AUGUSTINE

" In prayer it is better to have a heart without words than words without a heart. "

" To be a Christian without prayer is no more possible than to be alive without breathing. "

MARTIN LUTHER

CORRIE TEN BOOM

" What wings are to a bird and sails to a ship, so is prayer to the soul.

" You cannot pray for someone and hate them at the same time. "

BILLY GRAHAM

SIR

JOHN BUNYAN

SØREN KIERKEGAARD

" Prayer does not change God, but it changes him who prays. "

MOTHER TERESA

OSWALD CHAMBERS

" God speaks in the silence of the heart. Listening is the beginning of prayer. "

You know the value of prayer: It is precious beyond all price. Never, never neglect it. "

" We have to pray with our eyes on God, not on the difficulties. "

THOMAS BUXTON

→

Check out these insightful quotes and discuss them as a family.

PRAYER is Li

PUZZLE

Prayer is like a puzzle piece because it helps us to find our place in God's plan, just like a puzzle piece fits into a larger picture.

MAP

TELEPHONE

FLASHLIGHT

Prayer is like a flashlight because it helps us to see things more clearly, just like a flashlight helps us to see in the dark.

BACKPACK

Prayer is like a backpack because it helps us to carry our burdens and worries to God.

BREAZ

BATTERIES

AIRPLANE

Prayer is like an airplane because it lifts our spirits and helps us soar to new heights in our relationship with God.

KE A...

SOAP

UMBRELLA

KEY

Prayer is like a key because it unlocks the door to a closer relationship with God.

KITE

MIRROR

Prayer is like a mirror because it allows us to reflect on our actions and thoughts, just like a mirror allows us to see our physical appearance.

TELESCOPE

Prayer is like a telescope because it helps us to see things from a different perspective, just like a telescope helps us to see things that are far away.

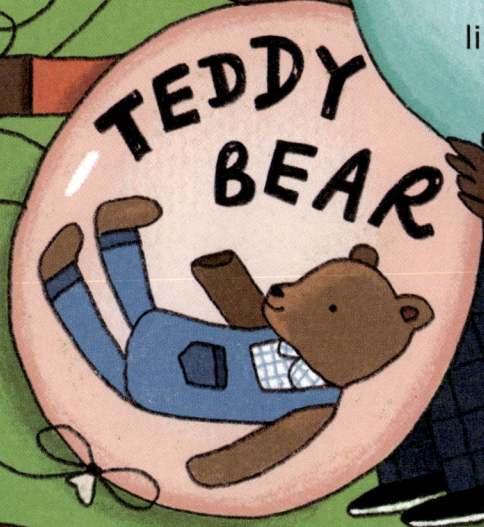

TEDDY BEAR

CHANGE THiNGS UP

Sometimes our prayer lives can feel a little stale and boring like we're saying the same things over and over again. It's totally normal, and it happens to everyone.

But guess what? There's a cool way to freshen things up! You can try praying from a different place, somewhere you don't usually pray. It's like having an adventure with your prayers! How about giving these new prayer locations a shot?

Place a check mark after you prayed at each location.

Underneath a big, shady tree. ☐

On top of a hill or mountain. ☐

On a swing at the playground. ☐

By a river, lake, or a stream. ☐

Under a starry sky. ☐

In the quiet corner of a library. ☐

Sitting on a tree branch. ☐

At a picnic table in the park. ☐

In a peaceful corner of a museum. ☐

In a hammock. ☐

Near a crackling fireplace. ☐

Under an umbrella during the rain. ☐

Inside a blanket tent with your stuffed animals. ☐

In a cozy attic. ☐

By a trickling fountain. ☐

So many fun options, right? Remember, prayer is all about talking to God, and He loves to hear from you no matter where you are. So go on, explore new prayer places, and have an amazing time connecting with Him. Keep your heart open, and enjoy your new prayer adventures!

BE A PRAYER HERO

Did you know that you have the superpower to help others through prayer? Yep, it's true! When we pray for someone, we're showing them love and support, and we're talking to God on their behalf. So, let's put on our prayer capes and become prayer heroes for others! Here are some cool and practical ways you can do it:

PRAYER LIST

Create a special prayer list. Write down the names of your family members, friends, teachers, or anyone who needs extra prayers. Keep this list in your room or backpack, and every day, spend some time talking to God about each person and their specific needs.

LIST
KATE
JACK
MAX

PRAYER CARDS

Make personalized prayer cards for people you want to pray for. Get crafty and decorate index cards with colors, stickers, or drawings. Write a heartfelt prayer on each card and give them to the person you're praying for. It's like giving them a little piece of love and encouragement!

PRAYER BUDDY

If you have a stuffed animal, turn it into a "prayer buddy." Each night, before you go to sleep, hug your prayer buddy tight and say a special prayer for someone who needs comfort, healing, or strength. Your prayer buddy will be like a gentle reminder to pray for others.

PRAYER PARTY

Invite your friends over for a prayer party! Sit in a circle and take turns sharing prayer requests. Pray together, supporting and encouraging one another. You can even have some snacks or play games afterward, celebrating the power of prayer and friendship.

PRAYER POSTCARDS

When you go on a trip or vacation, bring along some postcards and stamps. Take a moment to write a prayer on each postcard for someone you miss or someone who needs encouragement. Then mail them, and when the person receives your prayer-filled postcard, they'll know you're thinking of them!

PRAYER WALK

Take a walk around your neighborhood or school, and as you stroll, silently pray for the people you see. Pray for their health, happiness, and any challenges they may be facing. You're like a superhero, spreading invisible blessings wherever you go!

PRAYER HUGS

Give out special "prayer hugs" to your loved ones. When you hug someone, whisper a short prayer in their ear. It could be a prayer for their dreams, their well-being, or simply a prayer of thanks for having them in your life. Your hug will be a warm embrace filled with God's love.

PRAYER PHONE CALL

Make a phone call to a grandparent, relative, or family friend who may be feeling lonely. Chat with them, listen to their stories, and let them know that you're praying for them. Your call will be a ray of sunshine in their day.

Remember, prayer is a powerful way to make a difference in the lives of others. So, let's be prayer heroes and lift up those around us with love, kindness, and the mighty power of prayer!

Find these 12 objects in the picture: sock, alarm clock, dollar bill, soccer ball, teddy bear, apple, calculator, bicycle, doll, butterfly, toy dinosaur, paper airplane

LOOK & FIND

ARE U!?

PRAYING FOR OTHERS

Did you know that prayer is one of the best gifts we can give to someone? When we pray for others, we show them how much we care about them. Just like when you make a card or a drawing for someone, praying for them is a way to show love and support.

So here's a fun challenge for you: for the next 21 days, pick a new person from this list and say a special prayer for them.

ARE YOU UP FOR THE CHALLENGE?

LET'S GET PRAYING!

1 Pray for someone who inspires you to know and love God.

2 Pray for someone who hasn't been nice to you.

3 Pray for someone who is expecting a baby or is in the middle of adoption.

4 Pray for missionaries.

5 Pray for first responders.

6 Pray for local farmers.

7 Pray for foster care families.

8 Pray for the people who protect our country.

9 Pray for orphans.

14 Pray for local businesses.

15 Pray for someone who is living in a war-torn area.

13 Pray for the President of your country.

16 Pray for a friend that you would like to share the Gospel with.

21 Pray for someone who is sick or is in the hospital.

12 Pray for someone who believes in you and encourages you.

17 Pray for someone who means the world to you.

20 Pray for someone who is going through a tough time.

11 Pray for someone who makes you laugh.

18 Pray for someone who brings joy into your life.

10 Pray for persecuted Christians.

19 Pray for someone whom you've been overlooking and who could use some encouragement.

FOR WHOM?

Follow the lines to figure out who is praying for whom.

GARDEN OF PRAYERS

1 Grandma, I've always wondered how prayer works. Can you explain it to me?

Of course, Timmy!

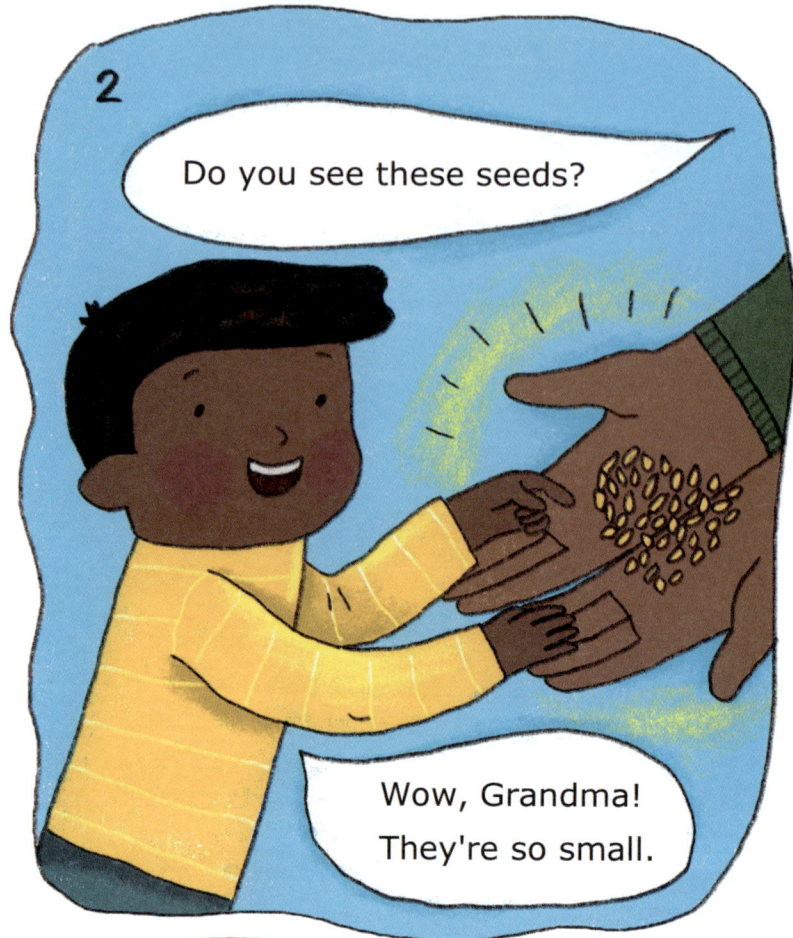

2 Do you see these seeds?

Wow, Grandma! They're so small.

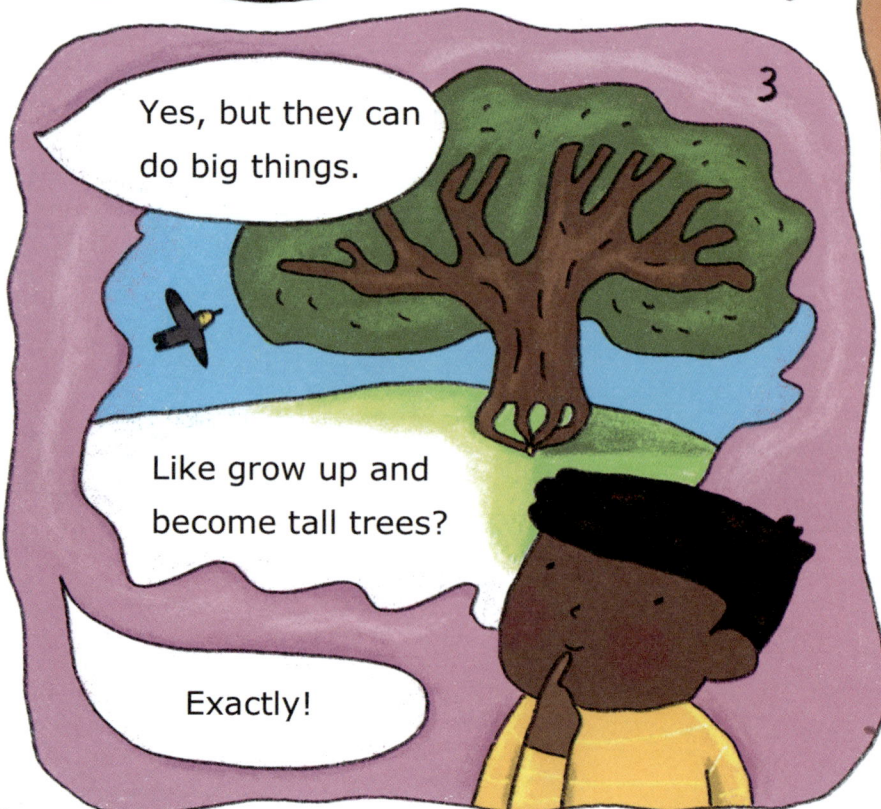

3 Yes, but they can do big things.

Like grow up and become tall trees?

Exactly!

4 Prayers are very much like these seeds.

How so?

43

14 These are weeds. They can hinder the growth of our flowers.

Just like worries and unbelief can hinder our prayers.

15 Let's get rid of them!

We won't let anything stop our flowers or our prayers!

16 Just like we take care of our garden, we should keep looking after our prayers.

And believe that God will make good things happen.

17 Thank you, Grandma, for teaching me about gardening and prayer!

Of course! Remember, prayer is a lifelong journey.

Keep planting your prayer seeds. One day they'll bloom and fill the world with God's glory.

MY PRAYER, PL

1 Write your prayer requests or praises on the leaves of this flower.

ANT

ARE YOU READY TO GROW YOUR OWN PRAYER PLANT?

2 For the next 7-14 days keep watering your plant by going over the prayers you wrote.

3 Keep your eyes open for what God will be doing in you, around you, and through you in response to your prayers!

LET'S TALK!

The coolest thing I have ever seen

The most memorable Christmas gift

Something I was crazy about but can't stand anymore

The most memorable road trip

One place I wish I could go back to

A lesson I learned the hard way

One thing I want to learn how to do

A time I felt really scared

My most embarrassing moment

A time when I couldn't stop laughing

The hardest thing I ever had to do

One thing I love most about myself

Find a penny or a dime. Give it to the player who'll go first.

That player drops the coin on the page, reads the t-shirt it lands on, and tells a story that fits.

The other players can ask questions about the story.

The storyteller passes the coin to another player. Play until everyone has shared a story.

One thing I want to change about myself

The best trip I have ever taken

The most interesting place I have ever seen

One thing I really wish I had

The best party I ever went to

A cool thing I once found

Five words I would use to describe myself

A time I felt really loved

A time when I felt really alone

My earliest memory

One thing I love about my life right now

PRAYER MOVES

Did you know that your posture and movement can make your prayers even more special and meaningful? Prayer through movement is a fantastic way to give your prayers deeper and richer expression by using various postures or gestures. It's like having a secret language between you and God!

For instance, when you want to show praise and gratitude to God, try raising your hands up high in the air. It's like saying, **"Thank you, God, for all the wonderful things in my life!"** You can even sway gently from side to side as you do it, like you're dancing with joy.

Now, let's say you want to ask for forgiveness or say sorry to God for something you've done wrong. Kneeling down can be a powerful gesture to show humility and honesty. Bow your head and close your eyes, and with a sincere heart, tell God what you're sorry for. It's like saying, **"I want to be a better person, God. Please forgive me."**

Sometimes, we all need comfort and reassurance. When you're feeling sad or scared, try hugging yourself tightly. This simple action can help you feel safe and loved. As you hold yourself, you can whisper a prayer to God, asking for strength and courage. It's like saying, **"God, please be with me and help me through this tough time."**

Remember, these are just a few examples, but you can create your own movements and gestures too! Let your imagination run wild and find ways to express your prayers through physical actions that feel right for you. You can twirl in circles to show happiness, sit quietly with your hands folded to show reflection, or even jump for joy to celebrate answered prayers!

So, the next time you pray, don't be afraid to move and let your body join in the conversation with God. He loves it when you talk to Him with your heart and your body. It's a beautiful way to connect with Him and show your love and devotion. Have fun exploring and expressing your prayers through movement, and may your prayers always be filled with joy, honesty, and love. Keep praying with your whole being, and you'll feel the beauty of connecting with God in a whole new way!

FAMILY MOMENTS

is a YouTube channel that uses really cool object lessons that teach the truth about what matters most!
It's fun, it's funny, and it's rapidly becoming the best family video devotional on the internet!
Check out our website at FamilyMomentsFun.com

10:36

100195

PRAYER INTERVIEWS

Are you ready to strengthen your "prayer muscles"? Just like we exercise our bodies to make them stronger, we can also make our prayers more powerful by learning from others. And guess what? One exciting way to do that is by interviewing people and learning about their experiences with prayer. So, grab your notepad, and let's get curious about praying!

Step 1: Finding the Right Person

Think about the people you know who might have interesting experiences with prayer. It could be your family members, friends, teachers, or even community leaders. They could be a grandparent, a teacher, a neighbor, or even someone from your church. Look for someone who is willing to share their thoughts and experiences openly.

Step 2: Setting Up the Interview

Before the interview, ask the person if they would be happy to talk to you about their prayer life. Explain that you are curious and eager to learn from their experiences. You could say something like,

"Hi, I'm really interested in learning about prayer, and I'd love to interview you about your experiences. Would you be willing to share some of your stories with me?"

Find a quiet and comfortable place where you can talk without distractions. Make sure to have a pen and paper or a notebook handy to jot down notes.

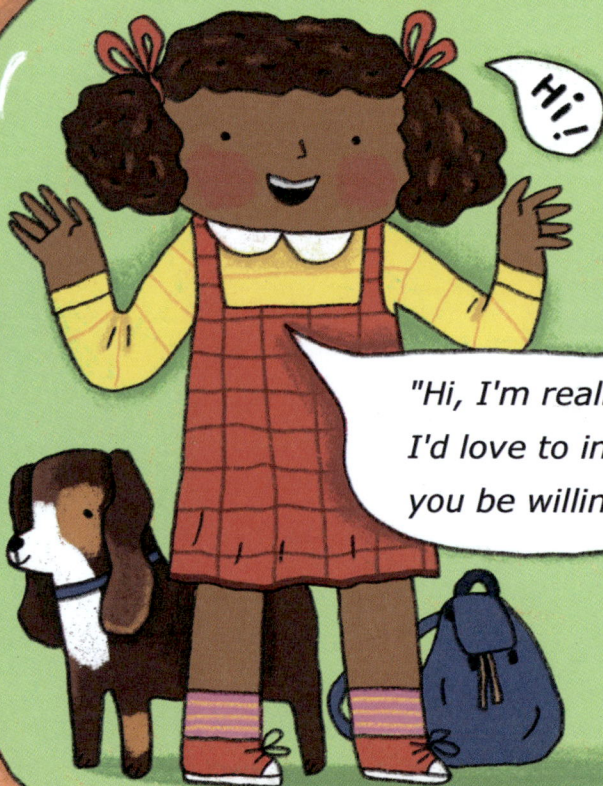

Hi!

Step 3: Getting Ready for the Interview

Take a few moments to think about what you want to learn from the person you're interviewing. Prepare a list of questions that will help you understand their prayer journey better. Here are some examples to get you started:

1. How did you start praying? Did someone teach you or did you figure it out on your own?

2. What do you usually pray for? Do you have any special prayers?

3. Have you ever had a prayer answered? Can you share a story about it?

4. Have you ever faced challenges or doubts in your prayer life? How did you overcome them?

5. How does praying make you feel? Does it bring you peace or comfort?

6. What role does the Bible play in your prayers?

7. How often do you pray? Is there a specific time or place where you like to pray?

8. What do you think is the most important thing about prayer?

9. Do you have any special practices or routines when you pray?

10. Have you ever felt like your prayers weren't answered? How did you handle that?

11. What advice would you give to someone who wants to strengthen their prayer life?

Keep in mind, these are just starting points. Feel free to come up with your own questions too!

WHEN I WAS...

Step 4: Interview Time!

During the interview, be a good listener. Pay attention to the person's words, body language, and emotions. It's okay to ask follow-up questions or ask for clarification if something is not clear. Make sure to thank the person for taking the time to share their experiences with you.

THANKS!

Step 5: Reflect and Learn

After the interview, take some time to reflect on what you've learned. Did anything surprise you? Did you discover any new ideas or insights about prayer? Write down your thoughts and feelings in your notebook.

MEOW

Step 6: Apply What You've Learned

Finally, take what you've learned from the interview and apply it to your own prayer life. Experiment with new ideas or techniques you discovered. Share your newfound knowledge with others who might benefit from it too!

Remember, interviews are a fantastic way to learn from others and grow stronger in your own prayer life. Embrace the wisdom of others, and let it shape your own prayer journey. So, go ahead and start interviewing! You never know what amazing insights you might uncover.

.LiE.
READING THE BIBLE AND PRAYING IS A WASTE OF TIME

.TRUTH.

As the deer longs for streams of water, so I long for you, O God. (Psalm 42:1)

TiME WiTH GOD TRANSFORMS US

Discover the joy of connecting your child to God's Word effortlessly and joyfully with *Truth Cards*. Explore the complete collection of cards at **WhatsforDinnerMag.com**!

TRUTH SIDE

LIE SIDE

TRUTH CARDS ♡

Enter your child's pain and stay there for a while

Praise God for who He is and what He has done in the past

Admit you don't have all the answers

Turn to Psalms and teach your child how to lament

Teach your child how to hope again

Pray for eyes to see what God is doing behind the scenes

Humble yourselves before the vastness of God's ways

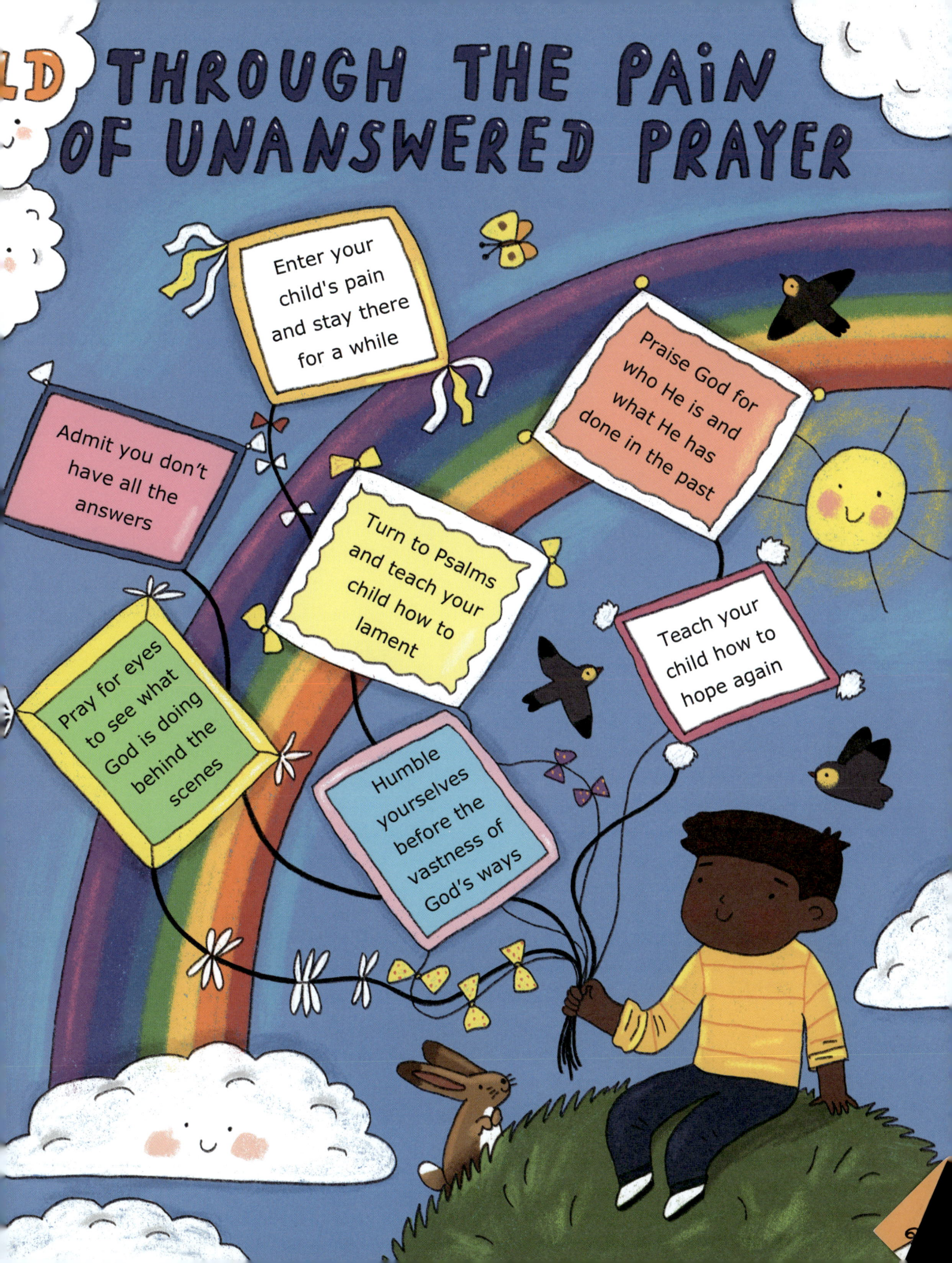

TRUE OR FALSE

Read each statement and as a family decide if it is true or false.

(T) (F) Prayer is a way to get God to give us what we want.

(T) (F) It is important to have faith when praying to God.

(T) (F) We need to use special words when we pray.

(T) (F) God always listens to our prayers, even if we don't always get the answer we want.

(T) (F) It is necessary to be in a specific place, like a church, to pray to God.

(T) (F) We should pray only when we need something from God.

(T) (F) We can pray silently in our hearts; we don't always have to speak out loud.

(T) (F) We must kneel when we pray.

(T) (F) Miracles only happened in the Bible and no longer happen today.

(T) (F) God loves to hear our prayers and wants to have a relationship with us.

(T) (F) We should always say "Amen" at the end of our prayers.

(T) (F) God answers every prayer, but sometimes the answer is "no" or "not yet."

(T) (F) Praying together with others, like family or friends, is a special way to connect with God.

(T) (F) We can pray to God about anything and everything, big or small.

(T) (F) It is important to thank God in our prayers for the blessings in our lives.

(T) (F) God hears and answers the prayers of children just as much as adults.

(T) (F) We can pray to God anytime, anywhere, and in any language.

(T) (F) Prayer is a way to show our love for God and deepen our relationship with Him.

(T) (F) God's timing is perfect, so even if we don't see immediate results, we can trust that He is working through our prayers.

(T) (F) Jesus taught us to pray in a model prayer called the Grand Prayer.